God Makes Me His Child

in *Baptism*

Story by
Janet Wittenback

Illustrations by
Janet McDonnell

CONCORDIA PUBLISHING HOUSE • SAINT LOUIS

*N*ow they were bringing even infants to Him that He might touch them. And when the disciples saw it, they rebuked them. But Jesus called them to Him, saying, "Let the children come to Me, and do not hinder them, for to such belongs the kingdom of God. Truly, I say to you, whoever does not receive the kingdom of God like a child shall not enter it."

Luke 18:15–17

Dad is calling. "It's time to go, now."

Today is a special Sunday. Today, my baby cousin, John, is going to be baptized.

This Sunday we sit in front of church.

The pastor and John's parents stand in front of everyone in church. Two other people stand there too.

One is holding John. They both answer
questions for him. Mother says they are his
sponsors.

The pastor makes the sign of the cross over John's head and over his heart.

I know Jesus died on the cross—For John's sins and for everybody's sins. We want John to believe that too.

The pastor uses a little dish shaped like a shell to pour water over John's head. He pours the water three times and says, "I baptize you in the name of the Father, and of the Son, and of the Holy Spirit."

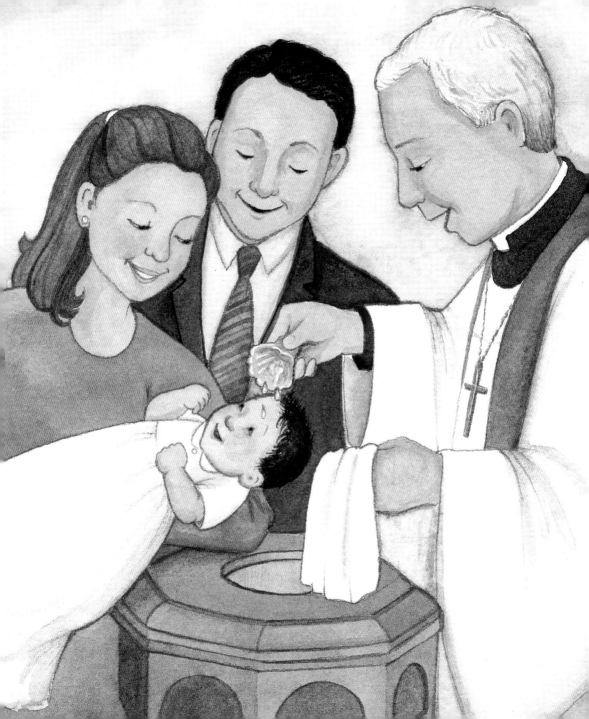

Mother whispers to me, "That's what happened at your Baptism too."

My sponsors are Aunt Ruth and Uncle Mark. When I was baptized, they said they would pray for me and help me learn God's Word and help me remember my Baptism.

When we're baptized, God makes us part of His family. It's a great, great, great big family. God's family lives all over the world. God's family is called the Church.

I'm glad Mother and Dad wanted me to be baptized. I'm glad they wanted me to be in God's family.

God wants me to be His child all my life—
when I'm little and when I'm big. God promises
to be with me all my life and to take me to heaven when I die.

He promised this when I was baptized. I hear this promise
every Sunday in church.

My whole family is in God's family.
We have fun together.

But, sometimes, I act as if I don't love my parents. Sometimes I act as if I am not God's child.

I sin.

But I am sorry for my sin.

God still wants me to be His child. God keeps the promise He made in my Baptism. God forgives my sin because of Jesus. God the Holy Spirit keeps me in God's family.

The Holy Spirit helps me remember my Baptism. He helps me remember God's promises. He talks to me through His Word, the Bible. He helps me try to do what God wants.

And He helps me love God
and Mother
and Dad
and everybody!

Lots of people don't know about God. I pray for them. I want someone to tell them about God. I want them to be baptized, too, and have God's promises.

God the Holy Spirit lives in my heart. He helps me praise God for His love. He helps me live as God's child. And, today, He helped me remember my Baptism. He will help John remember his Baptism too!